THE
LEADERSHIP
LESSONS

— OF —

Jesus

DEVOTIONAL
JOURNAL/PLANNER

BOB BRINER & RAY PRITCHARD

The Leadership Lessons of Jesus
Devotional Journal/Planner
© 1998 by Bob Briner
Printed in the Belgium
Published by Broadman & Holman Publishers,
Nashville, Tennessee

THE
LEADERSHIP
LESSONS

OF

Jesus

DEVOTIONAL

JOURNAL/PLANNER

And this was his message: "After me will come one more powerful than I, the thongs of whose sandals I am not worthy to stoop down and untie."
Mark 1:7

Who speaks for you? Who talks about you? What do they say? These are vital questions for every leader and every *potential* leader to ask continually, both of himself and of the quality of his leadership. What are others saying—to you, for you, and about you? It is safe to assume that if no one is helping communicate the message of your leadership, then no one is following you. If a distorted message is being disseminated, the quality and precision of your communication need attention.

What others were saying was important to Jesus. The powerful and fascinating account of John the Baptist underscores this. John, perhaps the most effective advance man of all time, sets a high standard for leaders to follow when choosing a spokesperson, one that should be upheld by both leaders and those who speak for them (which is itself a path to leadership).

The relationship between Jesus and John the Baptist demonstrates that truth is always the first and most important element of the spokesperson's message and that a quality spokesperson continues to speak the truth even in tough times when the truth may be unpopular. John the Baptist had powerful enemies, but he never cowered in the face of opposition. Today's leaders need to engender this kind of commitment in those chosen to speak for them. Jesus demonstrates a powerful way to do this; He appreciated John and highly honored him in public. If you are blessed with a loyal, quality spokesperson, don't hesitate to make your appreciation public knowledge—often.

Jesus was interested in what others were saying. Later in His ministry, in what may be an early example of public opinion sampling, Jesus asked His disciples, "Who do people say that the Son of Man is?" He followed this with an even more important question, "But who do you say that I am?"

Leaders need to ensure that followers help to disseminate their message, thus extending the reach of their leadership. Leaders need to ensure that those speaking for them are both truthful and loyal. From time to time a leader needs to assess the way his public—whomever they might be—perceives him. Most importantly, a leader must confirm that those closest to him understand who he is and what he hopes to achieve.

SUNDAY   Date: _____

_____

_____

MONDAY   Date: _____

_____

_____

TUESDAY   Date: _____

_____

_____

WEDNESDAY   Date: _____

_____

_____

THURSDAY   Date: _____

_____

_____

FRIDAY   Date: _____

_____

_____

SATURDAY   Date: _____

_____

_____

And a voice came from heaven:
"You are my Son, whom I love; with you I am well pleased."
Mark 1:11

The idea of a "calling," particularly for those not employed in some sort of professional ministry, is often seen as archaic, impractical, or quaint, even by Christians.

This view is damaging, both to God's kingdom and to individual lives and careers. As Christians, we must understand that God has a call on our *entire* lives, including our careers. To see this any differently denies both allegiance to God as our Creator and an understanding of the unbelievable price Jesus paid for us on the cross. It keeps us from living fully integrated lives in which all things work in synergy for our good and for the building of God's kingdom (for more on this, see *The Road Best Traveled: Knowing God's Will for Life* by Ray Pritchard [Crossway, 1995]).

Evidently, Jesus' leadership status needed to be reaffirmed by God the Father as Jesus began His earthly ministry; the voice from heaven saying, "Thou art my beloved Son; with thee I am well pleased" (Mark 1:11) was this affirmation. God has specific plans for each one of us, and we must do our best to determine what they are and submit to them. When we fail to do this, less than God's best often transpires. For example, a very gifted teacher at a Christian college—one *called* to teach—was railroaded into the college presidency by well-meaning colleagues, resulting in trauma, hard feelings, and disappointment on all sides. Gifts in one area, such as leadership abilities, are not necessarily transferable.

Never let someone else determine God's will for your life. No one else can understand God's unique call on your life as clearly as you. So many wasted years trying in vain to please others when they would be far more productive living as God designed them to live. This doesn't mean we go off half-cocked or without advice, but in the end, as Romans 14 says, each one of us must face God individually.

When we consider taking positions of leadership, we need to put out our fleece and seek God's affirmation. We may not hear an audible voice from heaven, but we can know that we are acting within God's will for our lives.

Week 2

SUNDAY   Date:

MONDAY   Date:

TUESDAY   Date:

WEDNESDAY   Date:

THURSDAY   Date:

FRIDAY   Date:

SATURDAY   Date:

At once the Spirit sent him out into the desert,
and he was in the desert forty days, being tempted by Satan.
Mark 1:12

Aspiring leaders must realize that the more effective their leadership, the more they will be tempted. The greater the ability to lead, the more powerful the temptations will be. A principal adversary for leaders comes from within—the temptation to abuse their leadership. Satan knew this when he put the greatest possible temptations before Jesus. You can be sure the evil one will come after you as you become a more effective leader. Knowledge of, and preparation for, temptation is imperative.

While temptation may lead to sin, temptation itself is not sinful. Rather, temptation—if successfully resisted—can reveal God's presence in our lives. Just as when the Spirit led Jesus into the desert, God may allow us to face potentially sinful situations that may be difficult for us to resist precisely so that we might develop godly character necessary for success in life, both on earth and in His kingdom.

Let's look at Billy Graham's example. He understood the variety of temptations that would be the most powerful for him and his ministry—lust, wealth, power, and pride. Dr. Graham built safeguards into his life and ministry to protect against each of these. To combat the temptation of lust, he continues to enforce a rule for his life that began in the earliest days of his ministry—never be alone with a woman other than his wife. Some snicker at this, considering it overly cautious, even silly. Not me. I see so many Christian leaders (both in business and the church) who have fallen because of sexual temptation—their effectiveness as leaders destroyed, not to mention their witness and personal relationships.

He also insisted that his evangelistic organization adopt the most stringent financial guidelines and that his own salary be set by a board of directors. Through the years his salary has always been extremely modest by most standards, helping to ensure that money did not dissipate the effectiveness of his leadership. The same board of directors that sets his salary helps Graham keep the attraction of power in check. He leads the board, but they have the final say in matters that effect the organization.

For many leaders, pride—a close relative of power—is the greatest of all leadership temptations. Looking good becomes more important than doing good. Leadership becomes the focus of the leader rather than the welfare of the organization and its people.

Accountability is the best antidote for pride. Billy Graham understands this, and is always careful to keep a close circle of friends to whom he is accountable. Leaders need to be held accountable. A friend or group of friends who will tell you the truth and help keep pride in check is a must for sustaining godly leadership over time.

Observations & Notes

SUNDAY   Date:

_____

_____

MONDAY   Date:

_____

_____

TUESDAY   Date:

_____

_____

WEDNESDAY   Date:

_____

_____

THURSDAY   Date:

_____

_____

FRIDAY   Date:

_____

_____

SATURDAY   Date:

_____

_____

_____

"Come, follow me," Jesus said,
"and I will make you fishers of men."
Mark 1:17

The difference between management and leadership is chiefly in the way those being managed or led are motivated.

In management, systems and techniques play a large role. However, leadership is characterized primarily by the way followers are motivated to please their leader voluntarily, and the leader typically possesses a more spontaneous personal style. Jesus was both the greatest manager and the greatest leader of all time, and both His management skills and leadership abilities should be prized and emulated.

In some ways His earthly leadership began when He called His first followers—Peter (Simon), Andrew, James, and John—from which the most important lesson to learn is that He *called*. He asked. He didn't just walk by, expecting some sort of supernatural attraction to occur. He called. He asked those four, who were to become some of His most devoted and productive followers, to "follow Me . . . ," a "must learn" lesson for today's leaders.

When you feel called to lead, and when you discover someone you really want and need to be involved in your endeavor, don't be coy. Follow the example of Jesus and *ask* them to join you. People want to be asked and feel needed. There is power in a personal call.

The current conventional wisdom relative to recruiting new business and professional personnel calls for focusing narrowly on graduates of the most prestigious universities. To be sure, Jesus, would have considered the Harvard MBA of His day or the top seminary graduate; after all, He chose Paul—one of the best-educated men of his time—and Matthew—skilled in the business of his day. Jesus' example in recruiting effective followers suggests that we cast the widest possible net. Consider everyone on his or her merit. Accept talent, character, and commitment where you find it. Do your best to look beyond the surface of family background, social status, degrees, and the patina of appearance. Real leaders look hard for real people with real virtues. Jesus chose followers from all walks of life.

As you lead and call followers, be sure you don't miss the most capable potential followers because you are afraid to go against the narrow focus of the world.

Whether your vision for leadership involves leading a godly family, leading a Sunday school class, developing a new product, revitalizing a lackluster ministry, or starting a new business, be sure you speak about it with fervor, frankness, and faith. Those you personally call to follow must be infected with your enthusiasm for the vision.

Observations & Notes

SUNDAY   Date:
_____
_____

MONDAY   Date:
_____
_____

TUESDAY   Date:
_____
_____

WEDNESDAY   Date:
_____
_____

THURSDAY   Date:
_____
_____

FRIDAY   Date:
_____
_____

SATURDAY   Date:
_____
_____

> *The people were amazed at his teaching, because he taught them as one who had authority, not as the teachers of the law.*
> Mark 1:22

Jesus taught with authority. In His presence, evil was repelled.

In an earthly sense, Jesus could teach with authority because He knew the Scriptures; He knew what He was talking about. But it was not just His knowledge of the Word that made Jesus the ultimate teacher. The Pharisees knew every point of the Law. Because Jesus was Himself the Son of God, His every word was absolutely authoritative.

Evil spirits were uncomfortable in His presence not only because He taught with authority, but because He was the embodiment of His message. He was the very antithesis of evil, and they could not stand to be where He was.

Leaders are *always* teachers. To be an effective long-range leader, you must teach with authority. You must be *prepared.* You must know what you are talking about. Remember, Jesus prepared for more than thirty years.

Be prepared.

As important as it is to know what you are talking about, it is perhaps even more important to be what you are talking about. Jesus could drive out evil spirits not because of what He knew but because of *who* He was. A leader's words, as vitally important as they are, will only go so far and impact so many unless they truly represent the reality in his or her life. A leader's call for commitment, integrity, dedication, and sacrifice will never be honored unless he or she is committed, honest, dedicated, and willing to sacrifice. Effective, enduring leadership calls for both precept *and* example.

A leader who speaks of what he knows and lives what he speaks will attract willing followers; those unwilling to be led will be so uncomfortable that they will be *very* willing to get out of the way.

Week 5

SUNDAY   Date:

_____

_____

MONDAY   Date:

_____

_____

TUESDAY   Date:

_____

_____

WEDNESDAY   Date:

_____

_____

THURSDAY   Date:

_____

_____

FRIDAY   Date:

_____

_____

SATURDAY   Date:

_____

_____

_____

So he went to her, took her hand and helped her up.
The fever left her and she began to wait on them.

Mark 1:31

A leader takes care of his followers and those important to his followers.

Those you are leading can only be effective when their needs *and* the needs of their families are met; an effective leader understands this and is sensitive to it. Serve your followers *and* their families.

This may sound "soft" to some hard-driving, goal-oriented modern leaders, but it is truly the ultimate hard-nosed formula for success. By removing obstacles to their focus, you enable your followers to concentrate on their given tasks. As strange as it may seem, the surest way for a leader to succeed is to put others first, including the families of those he leads.

Note that Jesus did not instruct one of His followers to help the woman up so that He could heal her; Jesus went to her and helped her up. He became personally involved in solving the problem—a small detail for someone with such an important mission.

It could have been argued that Jesus didn't have the time, but no one could criticize Him for not taking the time. Through this simple action, He proves that, although it is always easier to say, "Take care of this for me," it is often better to say, "Let me take care of it myself." Just as the woman Jesus healed acknowledged His grace by attending to the needs of Jesus and His followers, so will your followers and their families remember and appreciate your personal touch.

Observations & Notes

 Week 6

SUNDAY   Date:

MONDAY   Date:

TUESDAY   Date:

WEDNESDAY   Date:

THURSDAY   Date:

FRIDAY   Date:

SATURDAY   Date:

Very early in the morning, while it was still dark, Jesus got up, left the house and went off to a solitary place, where he prayed.

Mark 1:35

Mark is very precise in this passage, saying, "Very early in the morning, while it was still dark." Jesus disciplined Himself in the wise use of time; He was up and at 'em early. More importantly, however, He disciplined Himself to a time of prayer and solitude—prerequisites for Christians to succeed in any kind of leadership position.

A habit of prayer is perhaps more easily developed than a habit of solitude. Solitude must be sought diligently.

Solitude does not come naturally or easily. Mark says that when Simon and his companions found Jesus, they exclaimed, "Everyone is looking for you!" We would say, "Hey, what are you doing? Everyone needs you, and you are holed up in your office with the door closed." The fact that you are needed affirms your leadership, but followers must understand the need for regular periods of solitude.

Jesus' reply to Simon's exclamation is also quite instructive: "Let us go somewhere else—to the nearby villages—so I can preach there also. That is why I have come." Evidently Jesus was recharged and energized by the time of prayer and solitude, ready to move on and tackle the job ahead. Prayer and solitude do not cut into a leader's time or lessen his or her effectiveness; they add to and multiply that effectiveness.

Many of us have the wrong idea about prayer and solitude. In that sense, we view prayer as equivalent to a football team doing pregame warm-up drills. Everyone knows that the drills only get the team ready for the big game.

Prayer is where the battles of life are won and lost. We see something like this in Jesus' life. Again and again He gets alone with His Father and pours out His heart in prayer. Everything else that happens—the miracles, the teaching ministry, His confrontations with enemies—flows directly from His time alone with God. After all, the only place where His sweat poured out like blood was in a garden alone with God; He never struggled when faced with His enemies. He won the battle alone before leading His followers in the victory parade.

Prayer and solitude were vital to Jesus' leadership, and they are also "musts" for us.

Observations & Notes

SUNDAY   Date:

MONDAY   Date:

TUESDAY   Date:

WEDNESDAY   Date:

THURSDAY   Date:

FRIDAY   Date:

SATURDAY   Date:

Filled with compassion,
Jesus reached out his hand and touched the man.
Mark 1:41

The hard-nosed, knock-the-walls-down, slash-and-burn, victory-at-any-price kind of leadership always has its proponents; this kind of leader is often lauded—for a while.

However, enduring leadership, the kind that makes a positive, long-range difference, is always characterized by compassion. A compassionate leader cares about people, both as individuals and as a group. A compassionate leader simultaneously seeks the greatest good for individuals, the group, and the mission—not an easy task. What may seem good for an individual may not be good for the group or the mission. A leader must exercise compassion in a thoughtful, prayerful way.

Jesus proved that a compassionate leader need not be soft, sacrificing the group or the mission to protect the feelings of one person. Too often, Christian organizations do this in the name of compassion. I have seen trustee boards of Christian colleges keep a president in office when common sense dictated he should go, simply because they did not want to hurt him or his family. This is not thoughtful, prayerful, compassionate, or realistic. Although the feelings of the president and his family were protected for a while, the college faculty, several generations of college students, and all the supporters of the college—as well as its mission for God's kingdom—suffered.

Compassionate leaders care deeply about the feelings of individuals affected by their decisions, and they seek to deliver painful decisions in the most humane and caring manner. However, the greatest good for the group and the mission must also be considered.

Jesus showed great compassion when confronted with suffering. However, He often sent people away sad (as in the case of the rich young ruler) and—to accomplish His all-important mission—led many into lives of suffering, even martyrdom. He promised to show the great apostle Paul "how much he must suffer for my name."

Showing compassion sometimes requires breaking the rules, often in ways followers don't understand. In Jesus' time, touching a man with leprosy violated Mosaic law; according to the Law, Jesus would be rendered ceremonially unclean, thus unable to pray at the temple. Jesus' desire to help a poor leper outweighed His obligation to the Law.

SUNDAY   Date:

MONDAY   Date:

TUESDAY   Date:

WEDNESDAY   Date:

THURSDAY   Date:

FRIDAY   Date:

SATURDAY   Date:

Jesus sent him away at once with a strong warning:
"See that you don't tell this to anyone."
Mark 1:43

When Jesus came, He not only invaded space, but also time. Time and timing were central to His methods and His message. Everything He did was timed to perfection; the Scripture says that He came in the "fullness of time"—that is, at the perfect time.

Quality leadership demands a sensitivity to time. When we make decisions and when we announce them are sometimes more important than the decisions themselves. Timing is *that* important. I've sometimes delayed making and announcing raises and promotions so long that much of their morale-boosting effect was lost, a crucial yet common mistake in timing.

Premature decisions and public statements can be even more devastating. When the Chicago newspapers announced that Dewey had defeated Truman for the United States presidency before the final outcome showed just the opposite, they became the laughingstock of journalists everywhere. "Never early, never late, but always right on time" is an epithet any leader would love to have.

Jesus knew that a premature announcement of His miraculous power would impede His ministry, so He admonished the newly cleansed leper to tell no one of his amazing healing. It wasn't that Jesus didn't want others to know of His power, but that He didn't want to attract them for the wrong reasons. Scripture tells us that the leper could not keep the good news to himself; he began to tell everyone, causing Jesus to stay away from the towns and cities.

The fact that the people still came to Him "from everywhere" only proves that the attraction to Jesus was so powerful that even bad timing could not derail His mission. Our leadership undertakings are not that certain to succeed. Work and plan so that time works *for* you, not against you.

SUNDAY   Date:

_____

_____

MONDAY   Date:

_____

_____

TUESDAY   Date:

_____

_____

WEDNESDAY   Date:

_____

_____

THURSDAY   Date:

_____

_____

FRIDAY   Date:

_____

_____

SATURDAY   Date:

_____

_____

> *When Jesus saw their faith, he said to the paralytic,*
> *"Son, your sins are forgiven."*
> *Mark 2:5*

Leaders lead, managers manage. Often one person will fill both roles in an organization. Mark 2:1–12 introduces us to four men who did something all leaders must do from time to time: respond in a positive fashion to unexpected situations.

The four men who brought the paralytic to Jesus demonstrated both brilliant, spontaneous leadership *and* competent management. Many pure management-types would have been so discombobulated by such a novel interruption. Not Jesus. His brilliance as a leader allowed Him to respond in a way that made good things happen.

No other leader, no matter how brilliant, will have the supernatural ability of Jesus to know what those around him are thinking. But a leader must have the ability to evaluate a situation on the spot, to get a feel for what is taking place, and to make the situation work for good.

There in Capernaum, Jesus knew the thoughts of the people gathered in the house, particularly the thoughts of His adversaries. This knowledge, paired with His innate leadership ability, allowed Him to respond in a way that produced the greatest good. While much of this talent is inherent and God-given, it can certainly be developed and nurtured. Sometimes the talent is there, wasted by a lack of boldness. Many times I have understood a situation, known what I should say to accomplish the greatest good, but—ruled by timidity—I kept quiet. *Carpe diem*—seize the day—should be a key phrase for leaders.

Some people have the uncanny ability to be bold in negative ways or the propensity to say the wrong thing at the wrong time; they are the launchers of the proverbial "lead balloon." Because none of us is Jesus, this happens to all of us sometimes and should not deter us from developing and exercising leadership. He threw a question in their faces that forced them to think deeply. By challenging the paralytic to "Rise and walk," He established proof of His authority; everyone was able to check the results for themselves. Either the man got up or He didn't. Jesus not only forgave the man, but also healed him so that His opponents might acknowledge who He was—no humiliation, just a question to ponder long after the miracle was over.

A leader knows the difference between leadership and management, and values both. He is ready to respond in positive ways to the unexpected, consistently analyzing situations and responding with boldness as he is led by the Holy Spirit.

Week 10

SUNDAY   Date:

_____

_____

MONDAY   Date:

_____

_____

TUESDAY   Date:

_____

_____

WEDNESDAY   Date:

_____

_____

THURSDAY   Date:

_____

_____

FRIDAY   Date:

_____

_____

SATURDAY   Date:

_____

_____

> *A large crowd came to him,*
> *and he began to teach them.*
> *Mark 2:13*

Leaders are teachers. No matter what the enterprise—a family, school, church, or business—leaders are teachers. The terms are not interchangeable; not all teachers are leaders, but all leaders *are* teachers.

Jesus was addressed as "Rabbi" or "Teacher" more often than any other title, primarily by His disciples and the multitudes He taught. When the crowds came to Him, He didn't organize a pep rally or whip the increasingly larger and larger crowds into a frenzy with self-aggrandizing, flashy rhetoric; that is the way of a demagogue, not a leader.

A leader uses charismatic appeal, not only to evoke emotions but also, much more importantly, to teach. The power and cogency of the lessons are equally as important as the emotions stirred. In leadership, reaching both the heart *and* the head are important.

Many people are surprised when they first hear Pastor Jim Cymbala preach. Because he is the senior pastor of the ten-thousand-member Brooklyn Tabernacle—home of the world-famous Brooklyn Tabernacle Choir, which produces some of Christendom's most soul-stirring music—many expect fiery, flashy, demonstrative preaching. There is certainly nothing bland about Pastor Cymbala's presentations, but he is first and foremost a teacher of God's Word, relying on the power of the message—not the attractiveness of the messenger—to move his listeners to repentance and obedience. He leads his great church by teaching.

In this passage from Mark, it is not a coincidence that the teaching of Jesus preceded His call to Matthew. When the crowds came, Jesus began to teach, even as He walked along. Matthew undoubtedly had heard Jesus teach before in Capernaum, His adopted hometown. No doubt Matthew was moved to follow Jesus because of His teachings, not to discount the amazing appeal of the person of Jesus; He attracted multitudes, but those who followed closely and continually were those He taught.

When Jesus spoke those life-changing, history-changing words to Matthew—"Follow me"—he obeyed because he was moved by both the beauty of the Master *and* the power of His teaching. A leader attracts people to a cause and holds them with the power of his or her teaching. Only lessons well learned and fully internalized hold followers for the long haul; it is only these lessons that keep followers faithful and committed when the inevitable tough times come.

Observations & Notes

Week 11

SUNDAY   Date:

MONDAY   Date:

TUESDAY   Date:

WEDNESDAY   Date:

THURSDAY   Date:

FRIDAY   Date:

SATURDAY   Date:

*"Follow me," Jesus told him,
and Levi got up and followed him.*
Mark 2:14

My first jobs were coaching in high schools, long before I did anything but dream about the career in professional sports—that came much later. As a high school coach, I learned that when you have no paid staff and depend entirely on volunteers, it is *very* important to choose those volunteers carefully. One key to a high school coach's success is the student manager. A smart manager can be a coach's eyes and ears among his players in a way that no one else can. A good student manager is vital to running a good program.

A wise old athletic director—one of my first bosses—told me never to choose the most attractive, outgoing, or popular candidate for the position of student manager, particularly not one popular with the girls. Rather, he recommended selecting the smart but shy, introverted kind who failed to stand out in any area. His theory was that this type of kid (who had almost no friends and no other claim to fame) would be so grateful to you for plucking him out of obscurity that he would work like a beaver with unfaltering loyalty.

This great advice provided my teams with a succession of super student managers. My old athletic director could well have learned his selection theory from Jesus.

In choosing Matthew, a despised tax collector, Jesus certainly went against conventional wisdom, looking far beneath the surface of Matthew's unpopular profession to teach us quite an important leadership lesson: a wise leader builds his or her team very carefully. Choices are made *not* on appearance and appeal but on deeply, prayerfully considered values. One of the selection criteria should be considering who will most appreciate being chosen.

By choosing Matthew, Jesus showed that a leader should consider diversity when building his team. A less thoughtful leader puts together a homogeneous team of look-alikes who may also think alike because of their similar backgrounds and experiences—a much weaker team than one built with diversity in mind. We often think that diversity weakens a team when, in fact, the opposite is true. Jesus saw something in these men and wasn't afraid to choose them both for the same team. Only a great leader would risk that; only an extraordinary leader could pull it off.

SUNDAY   Date:

_____

_____

MONDAY   Date:

_____

_____

TUESDAY   Date:

_____

_____

WEDNESDAY   Date:

_____

_____

THURSDAY   Date:

_____

_____

FRIDAY   Date:

_____

_____

SATURDAY   Date:

_____

_____

*While Jesus was
having dinner at Levi's house ....
Mark 2:15*

Leaders eat with their troops. Food can be a great catalyst for building relationships and for teaching.

It is not just coincidence that Scripture so often uses food as a metaphor for knowledge and learning; bread, meat, fish, milk, and honey are all biblical synonyms for knowledge. The Gospels reveal how often food and drink are the backdrops for so many of Jesus' most powerful and important lessons (e.g., the Last Supper). They are spread throughout the New Testament, from the miracle of turning water into wine to the poignant way Jesus appeared to His disciples after the Resurrection as He cooked their breakfast by the shore of the Sea of Galilee.

Leaders do not neglect the power that food and mealtimes have to set the stage for building lasting, productive relationships and imparting important lessons. Leaders never forget how easily their followers can be intimidated. Nothing breaks down barriers like sharing a Coke and a hamburger or a quick breakfast together.

Memos, manuals, and seminars are useful instructional tools, but they can never replace the quiet lunch or dinner as a means of teaching, learning, and growing together. Private executive dining rooms and solitary working lunches may have their place in a leader's life, but the wise leader will be sure to "break bread" occasionally with those he seeks to lead.

Observations & Notes

SUNDAY   Date:

MONDAY   Date:

TUESDAY   Date:

WEDNESDAY   Date:

THURSDAY   Date:

FRIDAY   Date:

SATURDAY   Date:

Observations & Notes

> *"I have not come
> to call the righteous, but sinners."*
> *Mark 2:17*

Leaders must be able to face opposition with equanimity and confidence. The ability to hold one's own when faced with criticism builds tremendous confidence in followers.

Imagine how thrilling it was for Matthew and the other disciples to hear Jesus, with punch and power, respond to the criticism of the Pharisees: "I have come not to call the righteous, but sinners [to repentance]." Matthew and his fellow citizens must have been cowed and beaten down often by the haughty, law-spouting Pharisees. In Jesus they had found a champion to challenge these self-righteous hypocrites. By silencing the snipers with His potent response, He strengthened and solidified His leadership position.

Teachers can teach best in congenial settings conducive to learning, while leaders can teach even in hostile settings when faced with powerful attacks. Like Jesus at Matthew's home, leaders are prepared for the inevitable challenges.

Leaders know what they are talking about. They understand their mission and how to articulate it. We live in the media age, in which sound bites often are called for. Leaders must have their sound bites ready to inspire prospective followers.

Certainly Jesus taught in very thoughtful, comprehensive ways, as in the Sermon on the Mount and through His powerful parables. But very often He taught with what today we call "sound bites"—pithy, potent, precise comments that stopped the debate. Jesus was the ultimate counterpuncher; His opponents struck the first verbal blow, but He always struck the last.

SUNDAY   Date:

_____

_____

MONDAY   Date:

_____

_____

TUESDAY   Date:

_____

_____

WEDNESDAY   Date:

_____

_____

THURSDAY   Date:

_____

_____

FRIDAY   Date:

_____

_____

SATURDAY   Date:

_____

_____

*"And no one pours
new wine into old wineskins."*
Mark 2:22

It is not enough to have a new way of doing things or a new way of thinking, even if your way is better.

Change that ignores context eventually leads to anarchy. Leadership requires an understanding of newness in the context of the old; to put it more simply, a leader must know what is going on. He or she must also be able to articulate why the new way is better.

Truly innovative leaders will always be challenged by those who protect the old ways of doing things. Upon a closer look, these are usually the same people who are protected by the way things have always been done. Change always threatens some people.

Jesus brought more change and profound newness to life than anyone else in the history of the world. As a result, He was challenged at every turn, but He met each challenge with beautifully thought-out and cogently articulated responses, many of which constitute some of the most famous quotes of all time.
Think about some of them:

- "Get up, take your mat and walk" (Mark 2:9).
- "I will make you fishers of men" (Mark 1:17).
- "You are the salt of the earth" (Matt. 5:13).
- "Love your enemies" (Matt. 5:44).
- "Turn . . . the other cheek" (Matt. 5:39).
- "No one can serve two masters" (Matt. 6:24).
- "Do not throw your pearls before swine" (Matt. 7:6, rsv).

Never fall into the trap of thinking that because something is inherently better it will automatically succeed. Competent, compelling leadership must be exercised to ensure that even the best things endure. Sony's Betamax was, by almost all accounts, the best video system, Beta is long-gone. The leaders of Sony were never able to position their superior product for lasting success. Leadership failed to articulate why their product was superior.

Jesus never lost sight of His core values, and yet He continually evaluated the present context and adjusted accordingly. The change Christ brought always occurred within the context of the moment.

SUNDAY   Date:

MONDAY   Date:

TUESDAY   Date:

WEDNESDAY   Date:

THURSDAY   Date:

FRIDAY   Date:

SATURDAY   Date:

> Then he said to them,
> "The Sabbath was made for man, not man for the Sabbath."
> Mark 2:27

A leader has respect for traditions, but he has a greater respect for people. If a tradition is valid and helpful, a leader will use the tradition to help accomplish his goal.

Jesus did this in many ways, using the traditions that glorified God to help people understand Him and His will. However, Jesus was careful to brush aside traditions that were onerous or nonsensical and did not reflect the nature of God. Discerning the difference is critical.

A wise leader values those traditions that are useful in making people better and in making things better for people.

But traditions that inflict unnecessary burdens on people should always be a target for the effective leader. "We have always done it this way" is not a validating concept for a leader; a quality leader instead asks "Why?" and "Can we do it better?" When convinced a new way is better, a leader immediately begins to establish a new tradition, one better than the old.

When leaders must break tradition, however, they find a way to explain their new ideas in terms that followers can understand. By appealing to both the Scriptures and the account of David eating the consecrated bread, Jesus answered the Jews in terms they could understand. It's easy to say, "Out with the old, in with the new, and forget the past." But it is better to go "back to the future" by finding a precedent in the past for the changes you want to make in the present.

Tradition in and of itself is neither good nor bad. Wise leaders—especially those in established companies—must use the past but not be shackled by it. Tradition can sometimes become a chain if it keeps us from doing what needs to be done, which is what Jesus meant when he said, "The Sabbath was made for man, not man for the Sabbath."

Whether your area of leadership is in a home, school, church, civic organization, or business, how you handle the traditions there will help to determine how effective you are as a leader. A good *manager* makes the existing system work to his or her advantage; a good *leader* questions the system, making the changes necessary for improvement.

In Jesus, the ultimate leader, old things have passed away and all things have become new.

SUNDAY   Date:

_____

_____

MONDAY   Date:

_____

_____

TUESDAY   Date:

_____

_____

WEDNESDAY   Date:

_____

_____

THURSDAY   Date:

_____

_____

FRIDAY   Date:

_____

_____

SATURDAY   Date:

_____

_____

*Then the Pharisees went out
and began to plot with the Herodians how they might kill Jesus.*
Mark 3:6

A wise leader understands that no matter how pure the motive or how effective the action, there will always be those who oppose his or her leadership.

A leader should not be surprised or debilitated by opposition because it *will* come. Those not ready for it are often so stunned that they abdicate or resign their leadership positions. Some are not temperamentally suited to handle opposition, which comes even in the face of pure motives and quality, effective action; these people are not suited to be leaders because they are unwilling to pay the emotional price required when attacked while doing good. This is OK. Not all are called to be leaders. In fact, this is a good test of leadership: can you handle unwarranted criticism? Many can cope with rational criticism, but only a select few can both understand and effectively deal with the kind of criticism that has no logical basis.

Arthur Ashe was a great tennis star known for his coolness under fire. He and I were close friends for more than twenty-five years. The only time I ever saw him lose his composure was when he was the subject of an unwarranted attack by the very people he was working so hard to help.

As the president of the Association of Tennis Professionals, Arthur worked hard and sacrificed a great deal to help the players who were not the great stars, those who often lost in the early rounds of tournaments. In spite of all logic, these players verbally attacked Arthur in a pre-Wimbledon players' meeting, and the injustice and irrationality of the criticism caused Arthur to explode. Never again did I see him put himself in a leadership position that would subject him to that kind of direct attack. He learned something about his ability to lead in the face of unwarranted opposition, a lesson all potential leaders need to learn.

Leaders will be criticized. Good, effective, benevolent leaders are often criticized most. Be ready!

SUNDAY   Date:

_____

_____

MONDAY   Date:

_____

_____

TUESDAY   Date:

_____

_____

WEDNESDAY   Date:

_____

_____

THURSDAY   Date:

_____

_____

FRIDAY   Date:

_____

_____

SATURDAY   Date:

_____

_____

*Jesus withdrew with his disciples
to the lake, and a large crowd from Galilee followed.*
Mark 3:7

Even those who lead masses of people must have a small inner core of followers who receive special attention; a leader who keeps everyone at arm's length never accomplishes the maximum.

I know a college president—a brilliant educator, administrator, and writer—who (despite his great personal charm) was never able to develop close relationships with members of his administrative teams. Oddly, he seemed more at ease with crowds than in more intimate settings. He did fine work and represented his schools well. Although he accomplished a lot, he always seemed to move before he had completed his work and the most good could be accomplished. Insiders always cited a lack of close relationships with those he led as a reason for his shortened tenure.

Jesus made sure that concentrated attention was given to an inner circle of followers. Scripture tells us He spoke to the crowds but *taught* His disciples, saving some of the most important lessons for only three—Peter, James, and John. He often imparted more vital messages individually, as He did with His earthly brother James after the Resurrection, illustrating one of the most important and vital leadership lessons of Jesus: a very special, close relationship with a small group of followers is an *absolute essential* for the effective leader.

Concentrating exclusively on the masses rarely leaves a positive leadership legacy. A leader who imparts special insight and inspiration to a select few will have tremendous long-range results because those select few will continue to implement the leadership objectives in which they have come to believe. Consider the amazing results Jesus' disciples achieved *after* He left them.

There are certainly occasions when a leader needs to address the crowds. The effective leader works to develop skills, sensitivity, and comfort with crowds and small groups. While some are more naturally gifted in one setting than in others, it is possible to improve in both areas. If you aspire to be a leader (or perhaps a *better* leader), assess your strengths and weaknesses in each area and work to improve.

Observations & Notes

Week 18

SUNDAY   Date:

MONDAY   Date:

TUESDAY   Date:

WEDNESDAY   Date:

THURSDAY   Date:

FRIDAY   Date:

SATURDAY   Date:

> *Because of the crowd he told his disciples to have a small boat ready for him, to keep the people from crowding him.*
> *Mark 3:9*

Leaders instantaneously react to unexpected opportunities and obstacles, enabling them to maximize unanticipated situations.

This does not mean they do not plan. Visionary leadership requires both a long-range view of opportunities and short-range plans to advance to the next level. Measure your leadership by this. Do you have the ultimate goal clearly in mind? Do you know how to move to the next step?

Details are important. A friend once asked Michelangelo why he had labored so long over the intricate details of the Sistine Chapel in Rome, details so tiny no one would ever notice.

"After all," the friend said, "who will know whether it is perfect or not?"

"I will," the artist replied.

The passage of time has fully vindicated Michelangelo's painstaking attention to detail. Hundreds of years later his matchless frescoes are regarded as among the greatest works of art ever produced.

Is God interested in the details? Read Exodus 25–40 and study God's extremely detailed instructions for the construction of the tabernacle. He provides a blueprint any architect would admire. God cares about the details and so should we.

Jesus dealt with admiring and hostile crowds throughout His ministry, always planning for them. Whether it was telling His disciples to prepare a small boat for Him so He could be apart from them or leading them to a mountainside so He could more effectively address them, He always had a plan that complemented His leadership style.

Jesus' master plan is the most brilliant and awe-inspiring one ever conceived. He repeatedly demonstrated His leadership abilities through the precision of His planning. In even the seemingly small things, He led by planning; from the colt ready for His triumphal entry into Jerusalem to an upper room ready for the Last Supper, He made things happen by planning.

Follow His perfect example. Be a leader.

Be a planner.

SUNDAY   Date:

MONDAY   Date:

TUESDAY   Date:

WEDNESDAY   Date:

THURSDAY   Date:

FRIDAY   Date:

SATURDAY   Date:

But he gave them strict orders
not to tell who he was.
Mark 3:12

Observations & Notes

Strategic withdrawal is almost always a necessary part of success.

The wise leader knows that he will never go uninterrupted, undeterred from victory to victory. In every ongoing real-life situation there will be times when "discretion is the better part of valor," when a withdrawal, retreat, or time-out is not only necessary but *desirable*. The unwise leader can let ego, bravado, or wishful thinking make him or her forget that leadership in a worthwhile effort must take into account "the big picture." A lost battle or a strategic retreat in an overall winning effort is really a victory.

Sometimes you just have to yell, "Time-out!" If Michael Jordan needs a breather or Joe Montana needs to talk to the coach, we shouldn't feel badly about taking a break from the hectic routine to confer privately with our most trusted associates.

In both business and church life, I have seen worthwhile efforts end in futility because leaders were unwilling to strategically withdraw or take a tactical time-out, typically because of their excessive zeal or shortsightedness. In business, some executives invest so much ego in a plan, product, or program that they are unable to abandon a loser, even in the face of mounting losses and certain failure.

Some pastors and church leaders become so sure that their plans for evangelism, church growth, or a new building are on target that they insist on forging ahead in the face of congregational apathy or even outright opposition, unwilling to take a tactical time-out—to put things on hold—while they educate, encourage, and build a consensus. When this happens, churches are split, the plan—no matter how good—never materializes, and God's kingdom remains stagnant.

A wise leader picks his or her spots, retreating when necessary to accomplish the most good. Leadership often requires "taking one's lumps" and "biding one's time." Jesus demonstrated this leadership lesson for us so often and so brilliantly that it is one we should never forget.

SUNDAY — Date:

MONDAY — Date:

TUESDAY — Date:

WEDNESDAY — Date:

THURSDAY — Date:

FRIDAY — Date:

SATURDAY — Date:

*Jesus went up on a mountainside
and called to him those he wanted, and they came to him.*
Mark 3:13

Through Jesus' example we see that place is an important consideration.

It is not by accident or coincidence that Jesus chose a mountainside as the setting for His life-changing and history-making call to the twelve men who were to turn the world upside down—a memorable place for a most memorable occasion. Scripture does not tell us which mountainside Jesus chose, but, having been to Galilee many times, I can tell you that He had several awe-inspiring choices. Any of these would have provided a breathtaking, unforgettable setting for this pivotal moment in the lives of His followers. All leaders and would-be leaders should think very carefully about the setting—the place—for important occasions with followers.

Two occasions in my own business life underscore this for me. Before beginning my career in professional sports with the Miami Dolphins, my boss wanted me to spend time with the late Bill Veeck, who had become a legend as the owner of the Cleveland Indians and Chicago White Sox; his daring and innovative promotions provided the foundation for modern sports marketing and management.

My meeting with Mr. Veeck could have been held anywhere, in any number of very forgettable hotels. Instead, my boss wisely arranged for me to go to the Veeck home on Maryland's eastern shore. There, in his beautiful home beside the Chesapeake Bay, surrounded by a lifetime of memorabilia from a spectacular sports career, Bill Veeck spoke to me about the challenges and opportunities I would encounter with the Dolphins. This was a high for me, in part because the setting was so memorable.

When Jesus came, He invaded both time and space. As you lead, remember the great importance of both time *and* place.

Week 21

SUNDAY   Date:

MONDAY   Date:

TUESDAY   Date:

WEDNESDAY   Date:

THURSDAY   Date:

FRIDAY   Date:

SATURDAY   Date:

> *He appointed twelve—designating them apostles— that they might be with him and that he might send them out to preach and to have authority to drive out demons.*
> ### Mark 3:14–15

Leadership is largely about authority—acquiring it, using it, and investing it in others.

Leadership is *not* about issuing directives as a sort of traffic cop controlling the flow of action; that is a more managerial function. Leaders should attempt to replicate themselves, pulling followers along so that they can, more and more, act on their own to advance the cause. Visionaries anticipate the time when they will not be around, a time when followers must become leaders themselves if the cause is to go forward.

Jesus acquired authority from His Father, the power of His teaching, the uniqueness of His acts, and the force of who He was. He primarily used His authority as an investment in those around Him, teaching and inspiring them to act in His name, for His sake. That this was brilliant leadership is authenticated every day as millions around the world *continue* to act in His name and for His sake.

Leadership is lacking when it is not invested in followers in a way that empowers them to independently advance the cause. If a pastor is not producing congregation members who *can* and *do* "cast out demons," he has not learned, or is not appropriating, the leadership lessons of Jesus. A pastor may be a brilliant organizer and a compelling pulpiteer, but if none who attend his church are acquiring or using the authority that Jesus wants each of His followers to have, he fails the leadership test.

The wise leader brings together a group of followers who will give back to him or her. Mark says that Jesus appointed the twelve "that they might be with him." The cliché about being lonely at the top represents a leadership failure; the very best leaders are not lonely because they have developed an intimacy with a close group of followers. Are you producing a group of followers who are "with" you, who help to sustain you as you lead them?

Just as Jesus used special times and places to impact His leadership, He also used symbols in a powerful and compelling way. It is no coincidence that He appointed twelve apostles rather than ten or fourteen. The twelve represent the twelve tribes of Israel; the number has meaning and a message. Symbols are powerful. Give great thought to logos, titles, mottoes, and mission statements. They have significant and lasting impact. Use them as a part of your leadership strategy.

SUNDAY   Date:

MONDAY   Date:

TUESDAY   Date:

WEDNESDAY   Date:

THURSDAY   Date:

FRIDAY   Date:

SATURDAY   Date:

*When his family heard about this,
they went to take charge of him, for they said, "He is out of his mind."
Mark 3:21*

Withstanding an expected attack from enemies is one thing; even dissension among the ranks of followers, while no fun, is an anticipated part of leadership. But when our families don't believe in us, that hurts—deeply. Consider how Jesus must have felt on this occasion. He had pulled together a group of followers, performed miracles of healing, and attracted large crowds; yet His own family said, "We have to take charge of Him. He is out of His mind." That's a tough one.

Yet leadership at the highest level almost always demands such a compelling vision that even those closest to us may question our wisdom, even our sanity.

Contemplate this situation. If you aspire to leadership, see if you can pass this test: "If my family says I'm nuts, can I still go on?" Obviously Jesus did, but certainly not without pain.

It is important to realize that there is nothing disgraceful or shameful about failing this or any other tests of leadership; not everyone is called to be a leader. After all, for leaders to succeed, there must be followers. Most of us need to be good, dedicated followers in our earthly pursuits. In God's sight, leaders are not more highly valued than followers. He loves us all.

In my own business career, I think I was often at my best as a follower. I became the president of my company and was thrust into leadership responsibilities; but as I look back on forty years in business, I feel I was at my very best as a follower, as a number-two man, serving a leader I admired and respected.

There is no tragedy in failing to become a leader *if* we face up to the possibility of leadership squarely, honestly, and in an attitude of submission to God's will. If we prayerfully examine opportunities to lead and are then obedient, we will be successful as either a leader or a follower. Tragedies occur when we fail to take on leadership responsibilities that we are clearly called to fulfill, or when we pursue or demand leadership responsibilities without objectively and prayerfully examining our ability to lead. When either of these occur, people are hurt, resources are wasted, and good opportunities for growth are retarded.

Are you willing to pay the high price of leadership?

SUNDAY   Date:

_____

_____

MONDAY   Date:

_____

_____

TUESDAY   Date:

_____

_____

WEDNESDAY   Date:

_____

_____

THURSDAY   Date:

_____

_____

FRIDAY   Date:

_____

_____

SATURDAY   Date:

_____

_____

*So Jesus called them
and spoke to them in parables.*
Mark 3:23

The most effective communicators have been great storytellers, from Aesop to Jesus to Abraham Lincoln to Mark Twain to Garrison Keillor to Ronald Reagan. Why? Everyone loves a story. Stories are like windows to the truth.

In his landmark book on corporate leadership, *In Search of Excellence*, Tom Peters illustrates the effectiveness of leading by telling stories. Leading through storytelling requires more than just spinning yarns; the stories must make important, relevant points. Through parables Jesus imparted many of His most vital messages. Leaders need to appreciate this impact and prepare their own repertoire of parables that relate to their own particular enterprises.

Wayne Callaway became a very effective chairman of PepsiCo. I got to know him when we were both living in Dallas and he was running Frito-Lay, one of PepsiCo's biggest and most successful divisions. Most of corporate America attributes Frito-Lay's success to its legendary distribution system, legendary because—according to Wayne—the leadership of Frito-Lay very carefully, very deliberately told and retold stories of their distribution people going to extraordinary lengths to ensure that Frito-Lay products reached customers despite any difficult circumstances. These stories, told and retold, made heroes of those distribution people, made other Frito-Lay employees want to emulate them, and, most importantly, established a corporate culture that celebrated quality service.

Jesus both established and perfected the use of parables as a leadership methodology. Just think of the heroes He created who continue to inspire us—the good Samaritan, the good and faithful servant, the wise virgins, the poor widow, and others. As a leader, you need to teach through relevant stories that create heroes, build legends, and help establish the kind of culture that inspires your followers to excellence. Build up others through the stories you tell. Jesus was not the hero of the parables He told; others were. Too many tell stories of which they are the hero. Make others the heroes of your stories, not yourself. If you aim to be a hero, do what it takes to be the hero of stories others tell.

Jesus taught in many ways, but the wonderful stories He used are great examples of conveying important lessons in memorable ways. Wise leaders will take note.

SUNDAY
Date:

MONDAY
Date:

TUESDAY
Date:

WEDNESDAY
Date:

THURSDAY
Date:

FRIDAY
Date:

SATURDAY
Date:

"If a house is divided against itself,
that house cannot stand."
Mark 3:25

Quality leadership produces unity, and wise leadership is willing to sacrifice in order to build unity.

I had the privilege of being a college athlete. During four years of eligibility, I played on two quite different kinds of college basketball teams, different not so much in talent but in degrees of unity. Playing a long season on a team racked by dissension among players was not much fun and caused much of the joy of playing to be lost. The unified teams on which I played produced some of my most treasured memories and most enduring relationships.

Successful coaches often get rid of very talented players who cause disunity. The remaining players, though less talented, are often more successful. Unity means so much. There is no substitute for it. It is a prerequisite to sustained success.

Unity rarely just happens. It has to be sought and taught. In my basketball experience, the leadership that produced most of the team's unity came from a player rather than from the coach; the titular leader is not always the one who instills unity in his or her team. Conversely, unity can be easily destroyed by almost anyone. A wise leader does all he or she can to build with those who contribute to unity while eliminating the causes of disunity from the team.

When Jesus said that a house divided against itself cannot stand, He spoke a truth applicable to every kind of human endeavor. Unity is essential. Don't be afraid to eliminate the source of disunity from your enterprise—it's your responsibility as a leader.

Week 25

SUNDAY   Date:

MONDAY   Date:

TUESDAY   Date:

WEDNESDAY   Date:

THURSDAY   Date:

FRIDAY   Date:

SATURDAY   Date:

He said this because they were saying,
"He has an evil spirit."
Mark 3:30

Jesus showed us that even when we work exclusively for the welfare of others, some may say we are evil. In the instance Mark describes, the Pharisees deliberately twisted the words and deeds of Jesus to make them appear evil.

The same thing happens to leaders today, even to those with the best motives and the highest standards. You will never be fairly judged at all times. It is possible to do nothing but good and *still* be attacked. Don't expect fairness in a fallen world.

Winston Churchill was perhaps the greatest leader of the twentieth century. His magnificent, courageous leadership of the British people during the darkest days of World War 2 inspired freedom-loving people everywhere. Yet, in the first election after his leadership helped to secure victory over the Nazis, he was immediately voted out of office! This is an example of what leaders often face. Universal appreciation doesn't always follow great leadership.

SUNDAY   Date:

MONDAY   Date:

TUESDAY   Date:

WEDNESDAY   Date:

THURSDAY   Date:

FRIDAY   Date:

SATURDAY   Date:

> *"Whoever does God's will is*
> *my brother and sister and mother."*
> Mark 3:35

Leaders have special relationships with their followers and special responsibilities to them. When a leader beckons someone to follow, he or she asks to be responsible for an aspect of that person's life.

The life of Jesus and His involvement with followers demonstrates the intensity to which the leader/follower relationship can grow; it doesn't replace family relationships, but it can become just as strong. Obviously, the nature of the enterprise will dictate the intensity of the relationship. Coaching a youth soccer team is considerably different from leading troops into battle during wartime.

Jesus, the greatest of all leaders, clearly represents the special relationship that can evolve between leaders and followers. He never exhibited a cool detachment toward His followers; they were not simply pawns to carry out His wishes and implement His plans. His followers were very special to Him and, conversely, He was very special to them. This mutually caring, mutually productive, mutually protective, nonexploitive leader/follower relationship that Jesus maintained with His disciples is a model for all leaders and followers.

The idea that leaders should treat all followers exactly the same is a myth; trying to do this actually inhibits the kind of intimacy necessary for the most positive type of leadership to emerge. In order to lead a large number effectively, it is always necessary to have a deeper, more personal, more intense relationship with a small inner circle of followers.

In this passage we find that Jesus specifically called those "seated in a circle around him" His mother and His brothers. Although there is no doubt that He had a very special relationship with the twelve He called to be apostles and—of these twelve, an even closer relationship with Peter, James, and John—He really includes *all* of His followers in this intimate promise of a special relationship.

Good leaders have a vision; better leaders share a vision; the best leaders invite others to join them in spreading this vision. In this way, the best leaders create a sense of intimacy with hundreds, thousands, and even millions of followers, which explains why some feel that they know great world leaders even though they have never met. Shared vision binds leaders and followers together in a way that little else can.

SUNDAY   Date:

_____

_____

_____

MONDAY   Date:

_____

_____

_____

TUESDAY   Date:

_____

_____

_____

WEDNESDAY   Date:

_____

_____

_____

THURSDAY   Date:

_____

_____

_____

FRIDAY   Date:

_____

_____

_____

SATURDAY   Date:

_____

_____

_____

"Still other seed fell on good soil."
Mark 4:8

According to an old baseball cliché, "You win some. You lose some. And some get rained out." A wise leader will understand the implications of this for his or her leadership.

Every leader would like to win them all, but this is impossible; no one wins more than "some." It is also important to understand the "rainouts," those people and circumstances for which there will be another day; they are neither won nor lost, but will be in the future. They need to be remembered and "rescheduled" for the most opportune time and should not be written off or forgotten. A time will come for them. A good leader understands this and plans accordingly.

Because the sower couldn't know in advance where to find the best soil, he had to sow (e.g., "broadcast") the seed in all directions in order to guarantee that some would land on good soil. After all the marketing plans are made and the strategy is set, no one knows what will happen in the marketplace. All things being equal, however, the more you produce, the more you advertise, and the more you sell. The sower was willing to take a 75 percent "loss" in order to reap a 25 percent "profit," which actually yielded a hundredfold dividend.

Leaders who can't handle rejection, defeat, or delay don't last. Leaders who have to win everything *every time* are short-lived with limited success. Leaders must believe that if they sow good seed, *some* will fall on good soil. *Some* will produce good things. Even though they may not see good results immediately or even in their lifetime, Jesus teaches us that good seed *will* produce good fruit. We can't be discouraged by a lack of response, but we must trust God to bring about the harvest in His own time and His own way.

SUNDAY   Date:
_____
_____
_____

MONDAY   Date:
_____
_____
_____

TUESDAY   Date:
_____
_____
_____

WEDNESDAY   Date:
_____
_____
_____

THURSDAY   Date:
_____
_____
_____

FRIDAY   Date:
_____
_____
_____

SATURDAY   Date:
_____
_____
_____

Observations & Notes

*When he was alone,
the Twelve and the others around him asked him about the parables.
Mark 4:10*

To be effective over the long haul, a leader must speak the truth at all times. However, he or she may need to reserve some of the truth for those in an inner circle.

A leader's inner circle is defined by how much of the truth is shared with each prospective member. In the case of Jesus, He spoke to the multitudes and taught His disciples, but He reserved the most compelling truth for Peter, James, and John.

The truth shared with each group is very important in the way it is shared, in its content, and in its timing. The wonderful parables Jesus shared with the multitudes were undoubtedly carefully prepared, finely honed, and presented with precision and power, no less important than the message shared with His disciples, just different in degree. It's ironic that Jesus spoke in parables as much to conceal the truth as to reveal it, illustrated by verse 12: "They may indeed see but not perceive" (rsv). The parables are like a thermometer of the soul, revealing something of a person's spiritual perception (or lack thereof). That's why Jesus kept saying, "He who has ears to hear, let him hear." Not everyone has "ears" attuned to the truth of God, but some do. These quaint stories reveal as much about the hearer as they do the speaker.

When we set out to build the worldwide professional tennis tour, there were many competing interests. We had to carefully craft a message for the media to disseminate around the world; we had to articulate a more detailed message to the players of the world; and there was a very small, intimate group with which all of the plans and dreams for the future of tennis were shared. All of the messages were true and consistent, but each group received a different part of the truth at a different time. At the appropriate time all the interested parties were given all the available information and everyone knew all there was to know. The same is true of Jesus' message. He shared it differently, at different times during His time on earth, but now we all have equal access to it through Scripture.

A leader errs when he or she tells too much too soon to those not ready for it. A leader also errs by failing to assemble a small group who knows the very heartbeat of the vision and message. A wise leader will think carefully and pray earnestly about what, when, and how to release information.

SUNDAY   Date:

MONDAY   Date:

TUESDAY   Date:

WEDNESDAY   Date:

THURSDAY   Date:

FRIDAY   Date:

SATURDAY   Date:

"Others, like seed sown on good soil, hear the word, accept it, and produce a crop— thirty, sixty or even a hundred times what was sown."
Mark 4:20

The wonderful parable of the sower is a lesson about expectations. A wise leader will have realistic expectations about the receipt of his message and will keep the expectations of his followers firmly in check.

Jesus knew that even the very best message—eternal life as a gift of grace—would be rejected by most people, and He began very early to prepare His disciples for this. Unrealistic expectations produce disillusionment—a killer of any enterprise.

It's always important to emphasize the "up side" in communicating with followers. While keeping expectations real and preparing for the tough times is important, it is vital to show followers the potential fruit of staying the course, of being faithful to the mission. Both leaders and followers must believe in the thirty-sixty-one hundred multiple to persevere and hold steady.

We saw the parable of the sower played out in the construction of the Superdome in New Orleans. Without wise leadership this great stadium, which has proven to be such a boon to the city, would never have been built. At first, many saw the significant benefits of the stadium, but as the costs and difficulties were considered, many believers fell away. Some turned against the project as jealousies and greed were given free reign in their lives.

The two men most responsible for this huge project—Dave Dixon, who created the idea, and then-governor John McKiethen—could easily have become disillusioned and abandoned the project. As an assistant to Dave and the governor, I could easily have been discouraged as some of the state's major newspapers vehemently turned on the project, but Dave kept me and everyone else on a steady course.

The opposition, many of whom attacked him personally, did not discourage him, and he did not allow it to discourage me. Dave realistically expected opposition yet continued to articulate the benefits of success— the thirty-sixty-one hundred multiple. This is leadership. The result of this kind of leadership is a great stadium, one that will continue to benefit the state of Louisiana for decades to come.

Sow your seed. Have realistic expectations. Don't let discouragers discourage you—and enjoy the harvest.

SUNDAY   Date:

_____

_____

MONDAY   Date:

_____

_____

TUESDAY   Date:

_____

_____

WEDNESDAY   Date:

_____

_____

THURSDAY   Date:

_____

_____

FRIDAY   Date:

_____

_____

SATURDAY   Date:

_____

_____

"Do you bring in a lamp
to put it under a bowl or a bed?"
Mark 4:21

The Gospels have much to say about publicity and public relations.

The phenomenon of John the Baptist points us to the legitimacy of these activities when they are pursued in the best way, for the best ends. In opposition to the sincere, truthful efforts of John the Baptist (which were not self-serving or self-aggrandizing, but for the good of the mission) are those of the hypocritical Pharisees, who sought to portray a false image of what they did and who they were in order to gain undeserved praise.

Jesus wants the world to know who we are, who we truly are. A leader will understand this and make every effort to ensure that this happens by first ensuring that his followers know who he is and what he is about. Jesus did this by often questioning His disciples about Himself and His mission to be sure that their understanding constantly increased.

He also wanted the world to know the truth of His identity and His mission, employing the publicity methods of His day to accomplish this, starting with John the Baptist. If He had not hoped to disseminate His mission or message, He would have stayed in one place to teach His disciples. Instead, He traveled constantly, teaching and preaching in all sorts of venues to all sorts of people.

Several years ago, the Mercedes Benz automobile company ran ads describing a brand-new technology to help cars absorb the impact of a front-end collision. Although they owned the rights to the revolutionary technology, they freely shared it with other car companies in the interest of promoting safety. The tag line of the ad consisted of these thought-provoking words: *Some things in life are too important not to share.* In the same way, a leader must ensure that his "good news" isn't the "world's best kept secret." A wise leader will see the mission at the center of his efforts.

SUNDAY   Date:
_____
_____

MONDAY   Date:
_____
_____

TUESDAY   Date:
_____
_____

WEDNESDAY   Date:
_____
_____

THURSDAY   Date:
_____
_____

FRIDAY   Date:
_____
_____

SATURDAY   Date:
_____
_____

*"Consider carefully what you hear," he continued.
"With the measure you use, it will be measured to you—and even more."*
Mark 4:24

Effective leaders constantly evaluate their followers.

They must look for substance and avoid being fooled by the person who spends more time trying to look good than doing good. The larger the organization, the more difficult this becomes and the more important it is for leaders to discern the difference between solid performance and fluff. It is important to evaluate effort in order to give those who *do* perform added responsibility, thereby increasing their value to both the enterprise and to themselves.

Few things are more damaging to morale and to bottom-line results than failure of leadership to properly evaluate employees. When a person does an outstanding job without ever receiving bigger, more important, more rewarding responsibilities, it is discouraging. Perhaps even more discouraging is when leadership is gulled into giving credit to an undeserving person rather than the real performer.

Jesus tells us that he who is given responsibility and knowledge should use it productively, after which he should be given more. If a person does not use what he has, even this should be taken from him. To make this work—and it will work fairly for all—consistent, thorough, ongoing evaluation is necessary to ensure that each team member, as well as the enterprise itself, reaches its full potential.

Jesus repeatedly teaches that it is not how much we have that counts, but what we do with what we have. Leaders must help followers understand this principle and hold them accountable to it.

SUNDAY   Date:

_____

_____

MONDAY   Date:

_____

_____

TUESDAY   Date:

_____

_____

WEDNESDAY   Date:

_____

_____

THURSDAY   Date:

_____

_____

FRIDAY   Date:

_____

_____

SATURDAY   Date:

_____

_____

*"Night and day, whether he sleeps or gets up,
the seed sprouts and grows, though he does not know how."*

Mark 4:27

God is faithful. He expects all of us, particularly His leaders, to be faithful as well.

Just as there is order and consistency in the world God has created for us, there should be order and consistency in our leadership. We need to be faithful to our followers by articulating a clear, consistent message that states understandable goals and faithfully rewards those who help us reach our goals.

Nothing erodes a leader's effectiveness more than unfaithfulness. I know of a company whose leader constantly changes the playing field, earning him a reputation for unfaithfulness. He rigs the company's fiscal year results and employees' evaluation criteria to work in favor of the company's short-term bottom line, hurting everyone in the long run by his unfaithfulness. Employee turnover is high, and the company has been stagnant for several years. God's rules apply not only to the seasons—to planting and harvesting—but also to human relationships, business, and leadership.

Jesus teaches us that we cannot "beat the system." We may not understand how God's plan works, but we can know that He is faithful. We can know that if we lead faithfully He will bless our leadership efforts. We may not always "win" as the world measures winning, but as we plant good seed, a good harvest will result. Leaders are called to faithfulness more than they are called to success.

Observations & Notes

SUNDAY   Date:

_____

_____

MONDAY   Date:

_____

_____

TUESDAY   Date:

_____

_____

WEDNESDAY   Date:

_____

_____

THURSDAY   Date:

_____

_____

FRIDAY   Date:

_____

_____

SATURDAY   Date:

_____

_____

> *"It is like a mustard seed,*
> *which is the smallest seed you plant in the ground."*
> *Mark 4:31*

"Little Things Mean a Lot," might well be a theme song for leaders. More importantly, Jesus' parable of the mustard seed could easily be called a parable for leaders.

Leaders must understand that little things *do* mean a lot and that everything they do is magnified in the minds of those they lead. A follower's day can be ruined without a word of greeting from his or her leader. Conversely, a follower can be inspired and energized by the slightest positive comment from a leader.

Leaders need to be aware of the effect they have on those they lead. Successful leaders understand this and make their "little" contacts really count.

General Eisenhower spent the last few hours before D-Day mingling, not with the top brass, but with the soldiers, sailors, and airmen who were about to invade Europe. Don't become so preoccupied with thoughts of leadership that you fail to plant the "mustard seed" that will grow into a great, worthwhile relationship between you and those you lead. Be sensitive. Be alert.

Great ideas and great people have emerged from small beginnings. Seemingly unimpressive people can impact the world with the spark of a brilliant idea.

The Bible often celebrates small things. It was little David, not the giant Goliath. It was Gideon's small band, not the enemy hordes. It was the widow's mite, not the Pharisee's largesse. It was the cup of cold water in His name, not the grandstand play. Sometimes it's better to "think small."

Most importantly, the mustard seed parable is about faith. The most important faith any of us can have is in our Lord, who promises that even the tiniest faith can cause great things to happen.

In making a poor decision or in executing a bad plan, a leader will not destroy a follower's faith *if* it is apparent that the motives were good and that the leader was trying hard to do the right thing for the enterprise. Followers do not demand perfection, but they do expect and should receive honesty. An honest leader keeps followers' faith intact.

A wise leader will build faith in those he leads by giving individuals greater and greater responsibility and latitude as they demonstrate greater and greater capability and understanding.

SUNDAY   Date:

MONDAY   Date:

TUESDAY   Date:

WEDNESDAY   Date:

THURSDAY   Date:

FRIDAY   Date:

SATURDAY   Date:

He said to his disciples,
"Why are you so afraid? Do you still have no faith?"
Mark 4:40

A leader *must* be the calm in the storm.

Turbulent times are sure to come, and when they do it is imperative for a leader to be a calming, steadying influence. Many appear impressive when everyone is cheering, but a storm is always the true test of leadership mettle. Be ready for the storm; be ready to calm those around you in its midst.

Being the calm at the center of a storm does not mean being detached or unrealistic. It does mean moving deliberately and positively to handle the situation. Restate your mission to let your followers know what you are trying to do is both worthwhile and doable. Reciting past successes often helps rally the troops: "Remember when the wolf was at our door before and how we got through it?"

Visible, palpable panic is the telltale sign that the wrong person was given a leadership role. Working with the live telecasts of major sports events is tantamount to living in the eye of the storm. Many things can go wrong during a live telecast. The director is the leader and, in a big telecast, has hundreds of followers at his command, connected to each of his men and women by an audio line. If cameras go out, the satellite goes dark, or something goes wrong at the network, the director must control the situation by *what* he says and *how* he says it.

During a live telecast at the U.S. Open things started to go bad, and I saw the director, literally drenched in sweat, keep a voice as calm and reassuring as if he was at his grandmother's house: "Guys, camera three has stopped functioning. Give me some good close-ups with one," or "The Network is not receiving our feed. We will keep the tape rolling and give them the highlights when they are back up and running." No problem. Another day at the office. Everyone remains calm and the job gets done.

I have also seen the opposite happen. At a big event at Madison Square Garden in New York, I saw our director panic, rip his headphones off, and instigate a shoving match with one of the crew. Even the most experienced leaders sometimes falter under pressure.

Just as Jesus calmed both the physical storm and the storms in the hearts of His followers, leadership today requires the same kind of effort. We must *lead* through adverse circumstances, not be overcome by them. We need to control our own fears and repress any impulse to panic. Nothing will raise a leader in the eyes of his or her followers more than when he or she effectively handles a crisis.

SUNDAY   Date:

MONDAY   Date:

TUESDAY   Date:

WEDNESDAY   Date:

THURSDAY   Date:

FRIDAY   Date:

SATURDAY   Date:

*Then the people began to plead
with Jesus to leave their region.*
Mark 5:17

Leadership is a complex undertaking, involving both steadfast determination and thoughtful flexibility. An unwillingness to change (particularly a schedule) has caused a myriad of leadership failures. Quality leadership almost always requires strategic retreats.

Our company is involved in the production and worldwide distribution of television programming, beginning more than twenty-five years ago with tennis events. With its relatively long history of involvement with both England and the United States, Japan was a natural market for tennis programming. In the 1970s Korea was also emerging as an economic power in the region. My partner and I determined we would take our tennis programming there as well.

The Koreans had almost no interest in tennis, however, and no amount of effort could persuade their television executives that tennis would succeed in their market. In this instance, unlike some others, we were smart enough to beat a strategic retreat, returning to that market several years later and putting tennis on Korean television with great success. We were smart enough to adjust to *their* schedule, not try to force ours on them. When the Gadarenes pled with Jesus to leave their region, He didn't argue with them—He left.

Jesus showed us that it is sometimes necessary to "cut our losses," to change our schedule, or alter our plans. In Gadara He could have said, "Are you as demented as the wild man was before I came? I just worked a great miracle benefiting one of your own and, ultimately, your whole society. Don't you want to know more, to experience more of this kind of power?" He didn't. He left. He saw that this "market" was not ready and He left; He "cut His losses" and went into areas more central and more strategically important to His core mission.

Jesus exercised great leadership in refusing to be bogged down where returns would be small. Pride and ego didn't keep Him there. He didn't say, "I'll show them." Leaving a market, product, partnership, or business alliance can often be a critical strategic move. When we fail to make these moves decisively, it is usually because pride and ego impair our judgment. You don't have to let this happen to you.

SUNDAY   Date:

_____

_____

MONDAY   Date:

_____

_____

TUESDAY   Date:

_____

_____

WEDNESDAY   Date:

_____

_____

THURSDAY   Date:

_____

_____

FRIDAY   Date:

_____

_____

SATURDAY   Date:

_____

_____

So the man went away and began to tell in the Decapolis how much Jesus had done for him. And all the people were amazed.
Mark 5:20

Very early in my professional sports administration career I learned the difference between advertising and publicity, as well as their relative worth.

In the most basic sense, advertising is what you say about yourself, and publicity is what others say about you. Advertising is always discounted in the minds of those to whom it is directed. People intuitively know that advertising is self-serving and paints the best possible picture of those who buy the advertising, typically taking it with the proverbial grain of salt.

On the other hand, publicity, depending—to a degree—on the reputation and credibility of the disseminating organ, can have more of an impact. A favorable story in the *New York Times* by a respected columnist obviously has a greater effect than one in the *National Enquirer* by a writer of questionable integrity. Publicity—because of its greater credibility—is inherently more valuable than advertising.

The most potent kind of publicity is the first-person account. The person who can say, "This happened to me. I was there," is a very powerful publicity agent. Jesus put this publicity principle into practice when, after casting the demons out of the man, He did not let the man accompany Him but instructed him to go and tell his family how much the Lord had done for him. The man not only told his family, but also went into the ten cities of the region telling about Jesus and the mighty work He had done, thus becoming one of the all-time great publicity agents. As a living "before and after" example of the power of Jesus, the man was much more valuable in his home area than he would have been traveling with Jesus and the disciples. People who had seen him as a wild, naked demoniac could now see him clothed and in his right mind—and the man gave all the credit to Jesus. Powerful testimony. Powerful publicity. Powerful leadership.

It is vital that leaders understand the importance of strategically placing their team members. Jesus knew that the demon-free advocate would be a more powerful force for good in his home area than in places where he was unknown. Some leaders keep all their people with them at all times, a practice that hinders the spread of the Word and the growth of the enterprise. Do like Jesus did—place them strategically.

SUNDAY   Date:

MONDAY   Date:

TUESDAY   Date:

WEDNESDAY   Date:

THURSDAY   Date:

FRIDAY   Date:

SATURDAY   Date:

So Jesus went with him.
Mark 5:24

A quality leader acts decisively when the occasion calls for it—decisively, not impulsively.

In this situation, Jesus had all the facts necessary to act intelligently and helpfully. He didn't need to call a committee meeting or take a vote among His disciples—"All those in favor of going to help Jairus's daughter, raise your right hand." None of that. Neither did He tell Jairus, "I'll get back to you on that;" nor did He say, "Get me more information." He responded. He went. He moved. He acted. He led.

Jairus was credible. He was a leader of the synagogue, someone Jesus probably knew. He certainly made the right approach, one of great respect and faith. "So Jesus went with him." Great leadership is responsive leadership acting on quality information.

Great leadership is also courageous. When the news reached Him that Jairus's daughter had worsened and died, it would have been easy for Him to say, "I am so sorry. You reached me too late. I wish I could have helped." He didn't do this. When everything seemed lost, He continued to respond, act, and help. This is courageous and prudent leadership. Jesus *knew* what the situation was and *knew* He had the power to correct it.

No leader can do it all; in fact, no leader can do most of it. But good leaders understand the value of symbolic action. Jesus practiced this principle by "picking His spots" to maximize the educational benefit to His disciples. By accompanying Jairus, He showed His disciples that even the Son of God—*especially* the Son of God—has time for people who hurt, a lesson they would remember years later.

Obviously, none of us will ever have the wisdom, insight, or power of Jesus. However, He can be a model of leadership—in this instance, of responsive, cogent, decisive, courageous leadership—acting on quality information and continuing to move forward in the face of what appeared to be disaster.

SUNDAY   Date:

_____

_____

MONDAY   Date:

_____

_____

TUESDAY   Date:

_____

_____

WEDNESDAY   Date:

_____

_____

THURSDAY   Date:

_____

_____

FRIDAY   Date:

_____

_____

SATURDAY   Date:

_____

_____

_____

"Who touched my clothes?"
Mark 5:30

Leadership is expensive. As a leader, there is always a price to pay.

Just as Jesus realized "that power had gone out from him" when the woman touched Him in search of a miracle, potential leaders need to understand that leadership is a draining experience. Even as Jesus performed this wonderful act of healing, He felt the cost. The context in which this event occurs helps illuminate the cost of leadership. As the woman touched Him, Jesus was already on His way to deal with an urgent situation. As soon as He arrived He was swarmed by crowds and, after stepping ashore, was met with a critical situation that demanded His attention—only *some* of the costs of Jesus' leadership. The demands on your time and attention are very high, often leaving little time for yourself. But Mark's mention of the fact that Jesus felt power leave Him at the woman's touch is most telling; a leader does not, *cannot*, help others without giving of himself or herself. Leadership is costly.

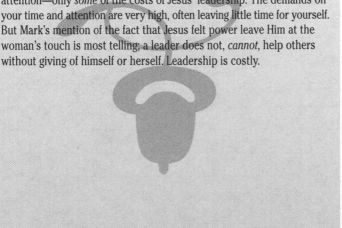

SUNDAY   Date:

_____

_____

_____

MONDAY   Date:

_____

_____

_____

TUESDAY   Date:

_____

_____

_____

WEDNESDAY   Date:

_____

_____

_____

THURSDAY   Date:

_____

_____

_____

FRIDAY   Date:

_____

_____

_____

SATURDAY   Date:

_____

_____

_____

He did not let anyone follow him except Peter,
James and John the brother of James.
Mark 5:37

Wise leaders plan for the time when they will no longer be around.

It is almost a business school cliché that a leader's first task is to ensure that the best possible replacement is being trained and prepared to step in when he or she can no longer lead. While the admonition is so logical and so frequently repeated, I am struck by how seldom it is practiced. Jesus, the wisest leader of all, certainly didn't make that mistake, telling His disciples almost from the moment He called them that He would not always be with them.

Unfortunately, even with the perfect example Jesus set for us and with all the leadership lessons others try to teach us, there are still far too many examples of huge vacuums being left as a leader departs.

Sadly, this happens often with churches. I know of one great south Florida church that has never been the same since the departure of its dynamic senior pastor several years ago; no plan for succession was in place, leaving a vacuum that remains to this day. You only have to read a current issue of the *Wall Street Journal* to find accounts of the same thing happening to businesses. Corporate leaders act as if they will always be there, and when the inevitable happens, no one is prepared to step in.

Christian leaders have a particular responsibility to plan for succession and the future of their enterprise. If they are to be good stewards of the leadership responsibility God has given them, they must do their best to prepare their own well-trained, experienced Peter, James, and John to smoothly and seamlessly assume command when they move on.

Thankfully, we also have some positive examples. Although this succession is still being played out, it seems that careful, prayerful planning has paved the way for Franklin Graham to gracefully assume the ministry responsibilities of his father, Billy Graham. It is fitting that Billy Graham will cap off his wonderfully productive life of service by following so closely the example of the One he has consistently followed.

Jesus trained and prepared the most successful leadership team of all time. Their achievements after Jesus' departure prove that leadership can be passed on by adequately investing in a plan for succession. Be a good leader. Be a good steward of your leadership by preparing for the inevitable time when you will no longer lead.

Week 40

SUNDAY   Date:

MONDAY   Date:

TUESDAY   Date:

WEDNESDAY   Date:

THURSDAY   Date:

FRIDAY   Date:

SATURDAY   Date:

*He gave strict orders not to let anyone know about this,
and told them to give her something to eat.*

Mark 5:43

"Visionary leader" can either serve as a complimentary description or relegate someone into the "dreamer" category—a person who sees the big picture but misses the smaller, important things.

Certainly a leader needs to understand and commit to a strategic plan, but big plans and brilliant strategy are always held captive to tactics and execution; if your alarm clock doesn't go off and you can't get your car to start, your big presentation on the future direction of the company might not happen. The ideal leader combines vision with the kind of common sense that makes his vision a reality.

Jesus was this kind of leader. When He said, "Give her something to eat," He demonstrated leadership through the completion of His thoughts. A lesser leader, after performing such a miraculous healing, might have done any number of things—made a speech, posed for pictures, or accepted the plaudits of witnesses—but Jesus said, "Give her something to eat." Fortunately, Peter, James, and John were present to absorb the lesson. After Pentecost, Peter—by then the group's leader—was careful to meet the more practical needs of the early church, while prayer, worship, and teaching moved the group forward spiritually. The best leaders are visionary *and* practical.

In this fallen world, the wisest, most successful leaders analyze their strengths and weaknesses and act accordingly. If you are a big thinker with the ability to visualize, make sure you surround yourself with people blessed with practical talent. If your leadership style is more practical, be sure to assemble a "brain trust" to complete some of the long-range planning and dreaming. It is not necessary for you to have it all, only to have access to it all.

The key is quality, prayerful, clear-eyed self-analysis. Don't convince yourself that you are strongly practical when you are not. If you fail to say the equivalent of "give her something to eat" when the situation demands it, make sure you have someone by your side who will whisper in your ear. If your style is to focus quite narrowly on the task at hand, be sure to have access to someone who thinks about tomorrow. This is the way staffs should be built—to complement the strengths of the leader and cover his or her weaknesses.

Don't be discouraged by Jesus' perfection. Don't be afraid to get help with those areas outside your natural strengths while working to improve areas of weakness.

SUNDAY   Date:

_____

_____

MONDAY   Date:

_____

_____

TUESDAY   Date:

_____

_____

WEDNESDAY   Date:

_____

_____

THURSDAY   Date:

_____

_____

FRIDAY   Date:

_____

_____

SATURDAY   Date:

_____

_____

And they took offense at him.
Mark 6:3

Leadership brings out both the best and the worst in people. Wise leaders understand this, accepting it as a natural part of leadership, and try to emphasize the best and minimize the worst.

Recognize that your motives will always be questioned by some and that, even when you are performing at your very best, creating the most good for the most people, some will "take offense." Unfortunately, those offended will often be people closest to you or those you have known the longest. Just as the people of Nazareth refused to see Jesus as anything other than a carpenter, in spite of the wisdom of His teaching and His miracles of healing, some will never recognize any leadership talent. Here is a classic example: One of Mark Twain's boyhood friends, jealous of the writer's fame, said, "I know just as many stories as Mark Twain. All he did was write them down."

When I was a young college baseball coach, my team played exceptionally, and I was named "Coach of the Year" in my state. One of my oldest friends celebrated my good fortune with me, while another remarked, "Being the baseball Coach of the Year in Michigan is no big deal. Michigan is not a great college baseball state." Some celebrate with you; some don't. This is a reality of leadership.

Recognize that you will probably be at your most productive away from "home." The old saying "take that show on the road" is one to consider; staying close to home has its comforts and rewards, but it also has its limitations and constrictions.

I have seen a lot of leadership talent wasted due to a refusal to leave home. Although it is good to have a strong appreciation and affection for home, returning periodically to visit as Jesus did, maximized leadership usually occurs away from home. Those who insist on staying at home often fail to fulfill their leadership potential.

Peter, James, and John did not become leaders by lingering in Capernaum on the Sea of Galilee, but by traveling to Jerusalem. "Come follow me" almost always means following away from home for maximum leadership effect, although there is nothing wrong with returning home if that is where the Lord has called you to be. For most of us, however, leaving home is a part of God's plan for our leadership.

SUNDAY   Date:

_____

_____

MONDAY   Date:

_____

_____

TUESDAY   Date:

_____

_____

WEDNESDAY   Date:

_____

_____

THURSDAY   Date:

_____

_____

FRIDAY   Date:

_____

_____

SATURDAY   Date:

_____

_____

*Calling the Twelve to him,
he sent them out two by two and gave them authority over evil spirits.*
Mark 6:7

Authority is *the* leadership commodity. How a leader uses his or her authority will help determine the effectiveness of that leadership.

Maximizing your authority is an elusive skill. Some try to exercise authority they have not earned and do not have, while others, paralyzed by fear or self-doubt, refuse to exercise the authority they clearly possess. Some leaders hold their authority too closely, strangling on the demands of the mundane and the minutiae of daily life. Some delegate too broadly, dissipating the potential effects of their authority.

Jesus appropriately exercised the authority He had. His was clearly not a democratic organization. When He told His disciples to prepare a boat to cross the Sea of Galilee, He didn't first call for a committee meeting. When He decided to head for Jerusalem, He didn't call for a show of hands to see how many agreed. He exercised His authority, yet He also recognized the authority of His Father: "Yet not what I will, but what you will."

In whatever the enterprise—a home, Sunday school class, church, or business—work hard as you lead to understand the extent of your authority, and then exercise it. Be the person to stop an appropriate part of "the buck." A leader, by definition, is a "buck stopper," one who makes decisions and accepts the responsibility for them.

A wise leader will naturally want to increase his or her authority if he or she realizes how precious it is. Authority can only grow if it is first given away, strategically delegated to competent followers. If delegated unwisely, it will be wasted on those unprepared for the responsibilities that accompany it.

Jesus delegated strategically. His disciples were given the theory *and* the practice. He was careful to send them out with a limited mandate. He gave them authority to cast out evil spirits, but He did not say at that time, "Go out and save the world." For the moment their authority was limited. Later it would embrace the entire world (see Mark 16:15). They knew what authority they had, as well as the constraints they faced in exercising it. Because of Jesus' wise leadership, authority grew, and good things happened.

Observations & Notes

SUNDAY   Date:

_____

_____

MONDAY   Date:

_____

_____

TUESDAY   Date:

_____

_____

WEDNESDAY   Date:

_____

_____

THURSDAY   Date:

_____

_____

FRIDAY   Date:

_____

_____

SATURDAY   Date:

_____

_____

*Calling the Twelve to him,
he sent them out two by two and gave them authority over evil spirits.*
Mark 6:7

Earlier in this book I mentioned my partner, Donald Dell. In the early days of our relationship, we learned that we were usually stronger and more effective as a team than as individuals. With this in mind, we were careful to handle the most important presentations and the toughest negotiations together whenever possible. When things of utmost importance are on the line, the two of us like to tackle them together.

We learned that two was the right number for us. At times, however, we decided to take along a third or even a fourth colleague—almost always a mistake. Donald and I worked so well together that two plus one was, for us, less than two. We developed a sort of natural rhythm together; in the give and take of intense negotiations, we almost never "stepped on the other's line," enabling us to enjoy many successes.

Obviously there were times when circumstance kept us from working together. I was the first American sports executive allowed into the People's Republic of China after the end of the terrible "Cultural Revolution," but a condition of my entrance was that I must go alone— no entourage, not even my partner, could accompany me. Though it was more than twenty years ago, I still remember how off-balance I was throughout the entire visit. I was not as effective alone.

As soon as possible, I worked out another visit to China—with my partner; we were able to negotiate some breakthrough business deals, among them the telecasting of NBA basketball games throughout the country. Through the years, we went "two by two" from Toledo to Tashkent and from Dayton to Dubai—wherever our business took us.

Jesus established the "two by two" *modus operandi* with His disciples, and, as you might expect, it worked beautifully. Scripture records that the disciples' success working "two by two" brought joy to Jesus, and He praised His Father for the effectiveness of His men. The effectiveness of the "two by two" leadership style is further demonstrated in the building of the early church, during which pairs of dedicated workers spread the Gospel and built the greatest organization of all time.

The leadership lesson is obvious: in almost every endeavor, the "two by two" system is the method to use, particularly when sending young people into a new territory for the first time; they will both learn and accomplish more together than they would individually.

Week 44

SUNDAY   Date:

MONDAY   Date:

TUESDAY   Date:

WEDNESDAY   Date:

THURSDAY   Date:

FRIDAY   Date:

SATURDAY   Date:

King Herod heard about this,
for Jesus' name had become well known.
Mark 6:14

This passage illustrates that, in a fallen world, in spite of how well or how often we tell our story and how well we react to things said about us, there will always be those who "just don't get it," who don't understand. They may know our names, but they don't and *won't* know who we are. This is not a reason to give up our publicity or public relations efforts, but, instead, it is a challenge to continue the work in hopes that some *will* "get it," some *will* understand.

Jesus' name had become well known, but even the king did not know who He really was. Others speculated wildly about who He might be, and both John the Baptist and Jesus Himself told the people who He was, but many really didn't want to hear or understand.

This is a lesson leaders need to fully comprehend, illustrating yet another cost of leadership. And the greater the success of leadership, the more misunderstanding and misinformation there will be, much of it personal. Just think of Jesus' own experience. He was and is the greatest leader of all time, performing many more miracles than were recorded in the Gospels; for more than two thousand years He has changed lives, inspiring men and women to do good. His Holy Spirit ministers to millions every day. To say the least, His name has "become well known." But still so many do not know *Him*, failing to understand who *He* really is. There is still much wild speculation about Him, even though we have the Bible—the greatest good news account of all time—and the Holy Spirit, an even greater teacher than John the Baptist.

As a leader, many may know your name. Few will know who you *really* are.

SUNDAY   Date:

MONDAY   Date:

TUESDAY   Date:

WEDNESDAY   Date:

THURSDAY   Date:

FRIDAY   Date:

SATURDAY   Date:

She went out and said to her mother, "What shall I ask for?"
"The head of John the Baptist," she answered.
Mark 6:24

Think of how Jesus must have felt when John the Baptist was imprisoned and then executed in such a horrible way.

Jesus knew, of course, that all of John's trouble—and ultimately his death—was directly related to His own mission. Jesus praised John as he did no other human, exposing the very special bond between them. Think of how that bond must have strengthened as John baptized Jesus, witnessing the blessing Jesus received from God the Father.

We know from Matthew that John's own disciples told Jesus of His death, the sad news driving Him to withdraw "by boat privately to a solitary place." But He had little time and little chance to mourn; the crowds came and, even in His time of grief for His fallen follower, Jesus had compassion on them and began to teach. A follower—the greatest of all followers—was lost, but the mission went on. The leader had little time to grieve, in no way indicating any callousness or lack of feeling on Jesus' part. His heart must have been broken, but His compassion for the living and the importance of His mission pushed Him on.

In analyzing our ability and willingness to lead, this sad episode in the life of Jesus provides another good test. Depending upon the importance of the enterprise, are you willing to continue to lead, to move ahead and focus on the future of the mission, even in the face of the loss of a devoted follower?

Week 46

SUNDAY   Date:

MONDAY   Date:

TUESDAY   Date:

WEDNESDAY   Date:

THURSDAY   Date:

FRIDAY   Date:

SATURDAY   Date:

*The apostles gathered around Jesus and reported
to him all they had done and taught.*
Mark 6:30

Many people have forgotten that the original owner of the Miami Dolphins—the great NFL franchise—was Danny Thomas, the wonderful entertainer and humanitarian. Many of us who joined in the effort to build the franchise were attracted to the enterprise by the opportunity to work for him. The Atlanta Falcons came into existence the same year, but for me the Dolphins were more appealing because of Danny Thomas.

Danny lived in Hollywood and only came to Miami periodically. When he did, it was an exciting time for those who constituted the Dolphins' first office staff. We were eager to report to him all that we were doing to build the team and franchise; however, he was sometimes too busy to see all of us during his brief visit, and, thirty years later, I still remember how disappointed I was when he was unable to meet with me. He was my leader, and I wanted to report to him.

As you lead, the idea to have your people report to you in written form may seem to be a good one: you can peruse the reports as you have the time to do so; you have a written record of your workers' activities; and you are able to jot appropriate notes back—all very neat and orderly, but so much is lost. A wise leader does not rely solely on notes and memos to communicate with those he leads; he makes certain to allow for time to "lead by walking around" (to use a Tom Peters phrase). He or she sees and is seen by those doing the work, and this is important so that team members can receive regular personal time from and easy access to their leader whenever necessary.

When His disciples returned from the successful mission on which Jesus sent them, one which enabled them to practice many of the things He had told them, can you imagine how eager they were to report to Him? This must have been a joyful, energizing time.
As you lead, don't waste valuable opportunities to lead by saying, "Just send me a note on that." Take Jesus' lead—gather your people around you and let them tell you "all they [have] done and taught."

SUNDAY   Date:

_____

_____

MONDAY   Date:

_____

_____

TUESDAY   Date:

_____

_____

WEDNESDAY   Date:

_____

_____

THURSDAY   Date:

_____

_____

FRIDAY   Date:

_____

_____

SATURDAY   Date:

_____

_____

_____

*Then, because so many people were coming and going that
they did not even have a chance to eat, he said to them,
"Come with me by yourselves to a quiet place and get some rest."
Mark 6:31*

In the above verse, Jesus lays out all the directions necessary for a productive leadership retreat—corporate, church, or family.

During more than forty years in business, I have been to my share of leadership retreats, the most productive of which followed the simple guidelines laid down for us by Jesus. When we deviated from those, our company retreats were less productive than they might have been.

One of the temptations we sometimes find hard to resist is planning a retreat that allows time to "get a little work done." This sounds like a contradiction in terms—a retreat where work is done—but at our corporate retreats and at Christian college board retreats, there is often some work built into the agenda, usually a mistake. Jesus said, "Get some rest," which should be the primary purpose of a retreat.

We scheduled several past retreats in a big city or a theme park setting as a way of rewarding our employees. *Big* mistake. It is sometimes productive to reward *individual* employees and their families with a trip, but a retreat should be like the one Jesus proposed for His disciples—in a "quiet place."

Another common mistake is to bring in numerous speakers to a corporate retreat setting. Certainly there is a time for consultants, outside experts, and inspirational speakers. However, every enterprise should have at least one yearly retreat to which the leader's invitation should say, "Come with me by yourselves." A wise leader will always schedule time with followers that excludes outsiders. These are times of great importance and significance and should not be missed.

Observations & Notes

Week 48

SUNDAY   Date:

MONDAY   Date:

TUESDAY   Date:

WEDNESDAY   Date:

THURSDAY   Date:

FRIDAY   Date:

SATURDAY   Date:

When Jesus landed and saw a large crowd,
he had compassion on them,
because they were like sheep without a shepherd.
So he began teaching them many things.
Mark 6:34

Wise leaders will always have a schedule, a plan to use time most productively, but the wisest leader will never make it his master.

Important but unplanned moments periodically occur that should not be lost, even though they disrupt a planned schedule. One of the tensions of leadership is finding the proper balance between adhering to a well-planned schedule and being flexible enough not to lose those spontaneous opportunities that cross our paths. This is not easy. I have seen both extremes.

Some leaders seem to career from one unplanned event to another, their schedules meaning nothing. I know of one corporation chairman whose company has been severely damaged because of his failure to keep any sort of schedule, resulting in broken relationships, severed alliances, and lost business opportunities. At the other extreme, I have seen leaders who rarely deviated from a planned schedule, resulting in many missed opportunities. Both extremes are examples of ineffective leadership.

How do we find a balance? Jesus had a plan, one which He moved inexorably to accomplish. But as He did so, He utilized those special, unplanned occasions to contribute to the successful conclusion of His original plan. By following a schedule until and unless those special opportunities arise that will make the overall goal more attainable, you will maintain a schedule that works for you and your organization.

As in the above passage, compassion was typically Jesus' motivation for deviating from His schedule. Compassion may not seem useful for today's leaders in intense business situations, but consider this: a concern for the welfare of people rarely leads us to an unprofitable or unproductive use of our time. Wise compassion, the kind that moved Jesus, does not cause a leader to become so weak that he damages the enterprise or hurts those around him. Rather, it is a clear-headed emotion that enables us to strive to accomplish the most good for the most people. Sometimes this is achieved by closely adhering to a schedule. Sometimes it is achieved by being flexible and taking compassionate detours that help to accomplish your overall goal.

When thinking about your schedule, remember how Jesus approached His.

Observations & Notes

SUNDAY   Date:

MONDAY   Date:

TUESDAY   Date:

WEDNESDAY   Date:

THURSDAY   Date:

FRIDAY   Date:

SATURDAY   Date:

*But he answered,
"You give them something to eat."*
Mark 6:37

Boldness builds leadership, but rashness destroys it. Discerning between the two is critical.

My life and business career have been blessed by associations with bold leaders. Among those, David F. Dixon stands out as perhaps the boldest. I can still remember when he said, "Bob, we are going to build the world's greatest stadium, and we are going to build it in downtown New Orleans."

Sure, Dave. I ticked off the problems in my head. Louisiana is an unlikely place for the world's largest stadium. New Orleans is among the smallest television markets. And to top it off, I knew that voters in the northern part of the state rarely supported projects in New Orleans. None of that deterred Dave Dixon from following through with his vision, and the Superdome in New Orleans stands as a monument to his boldness.

When Jesus told the disciples to feed the five thousand, it was among His boldest leadership moves, but it wasn't rash. He knew He could make it happen; it was His shortsighted disciples who saw only the crowds.

By saying "You feed them," Jesus did three things every leader must do: (1) He imparted a vision that only He could see; (2) He delegated full authority to His subordinates to accomplish the task at hand; and (3) He allowed them to share fully in the fulfillment of the vision.

When Dave Dixon told me that we were going to build a great domed stadium in downtown New Orleans, it was also a bold—not a rash—statement, one that reflected a bold vision. Although he certainly did not have the perfect foresight of Jesus, Dave "knew" we were going to build the stadium. This kind of knowledge is called leadership—*bold* leadership.

In the home, in our churches, in business, and in education, people thirst for bold leadership. People follow bold leaders. The feeding of the five thousand contributed to the boldness ultimately displayed by the disciples as they faced and conquered every obstacle they encountered in their quest to spread the gospel. The benefits of bold leadership continue even after the leader has disappeared from the scene.

Jesus is the greatest and boldest of all leaders. His followers, particularly those in positions of leadership today, need to view boldness as the norm, not as an elusive, extraordinary leadership style.

SUNDAY   Date:

_____

_____

MONDAY   Date:

_____

_____

TUESDAY   Date:

_____

_____

WEDNESDAY   Date:

_____

_____

THURSDAY   Date:

_____

_____

FRIDAY   Date:

_____

_____

SATURDAY   Date:

_____

_____

Then Jesus directed them to have all the people
sit down in groups on the green grass.
Mark 6:39

One of a leader's first responsibilities is to establish order.

We serve a God of order. A significant function of His act of Creation was to bring order out of chaos. Before Jesus fed the five thousand, He instructed the disciples to organize the crowd. In fact, His compassion for them was triggered by their lack of order: "They were like sheep without a shepherd."

Moving into any situation, an effective leader begins by creating order. Don't mistake a martinet for a leader. A martinet does create order, but only for the sense of power and control it gives him. A leader creates order so he or she can more effectively serve others. Jesus encouraged the people to sit in groups so that He and the disciples could better serve them. For a leader, order is never merely an exercise of power, but a necessary part of preparation for service.

Contrary to popular opinion, order does not stifle creativity, but promotes it. It does not restrict freedom, but enhances it for the greatest number. Disorder is a kind of tyranny in which good things seldom happen. When disorder reigns, people suffer in many ways.

There is a vast difference between order and regimentation. Jesus didn't tell the five thousand to sit down in groups, organized alphabetically by last name, to count off, and remain silent until addressed. Instead, He created an order that was not ominous and restrictive, but pleasant and liberating. Regimentation stifles creativity and restricts freedom, but order creates an environment where freedom and creativity flourish.

Week 51

SUNDAY   Date:

MONDAY   Date:

TUESDAY   Date:

WEDNESDAY   Date:

THURSDAY   Date:

FRIDAY   Date:

SATURDAY   Date:

After leaving them,
he went up on a mountainside to pray.
Mark 6:46

This short passage of only seven verses contains many leadership lessons, the key one being that prayer is as necessary after triumph as it is before difficulty.

Our tendency is to pray when facing peril, but to forget prayer after God has seen us through hard times. Jesus prayed before feeding the five thousand as He gave thanks for the bread; but even more significantly, *after* the great miracle and *after* dismissing the crowd and sending His disciples away, "he went up on a mountainside to pray." This is a great lesson for everyone who leads.

Time alone, time in *prayer* alone, is necessary for successful leadership. Certainly, prayer is important as we look toward the inevitable difficulties we will face, but Jesus shows us that it is also vital *after* God has allowed our leadership to succeed. These times of prayer strengthen and sustain us—perhaps more than any other—and should be the most joyful and memorable times of praise, worship, and celebration of our wonderful heavenly Father; times for thanks and thanksgiving, and times of expressing love and adoration. The only petitioning in these times of prayer should be for the grace to love Him more.

After He has seen us—or allowed us to lead others—through difficulty, we should be certain to go to Him in prayer. This is not a time for casual prayer that we whisper as we move on to our next activity. Jesus could easily have gone with His disciples as they left for Bethsaida, which would have been the natural, expected thing to do. Why wait and travel alone? Because God's great help and great blessing demanded a particularly meaningful time of communion with Him.

As a leader today, with the knowledge of the scriptural account, the great joy of knowing Jesus, and access to the help of the Holy Spirit, it is even more important that we express our thanks after times of help, blessing, and triumph. Doing this will allow us to approach our Father more confidently when we again need His help in facing a difficult situation. How can we go to Him with another petition when we did not thank Him or worship Him when He first provided for us?

The best leaders are also the most thankful people on earth because they realize that everything they have is a gift from God. Be thankful and remember the One from whom all blessings flow.

God bless you as you lead in your home, church, and business. Continue to look to Jesus, our ultimate leader.

Observations & Notes

SUNDAY   Date:

_____

_____

MONDAY   Date:

_____

_____

TUESDAY   Date:

_____

_____

WEDNESDAY   Date:

_____

_____

THURSDAY   Date:

_____

_____

FRIDAY   Date:

_____

_____

SATURDAY   Date:

_____

_____

Personal Notes

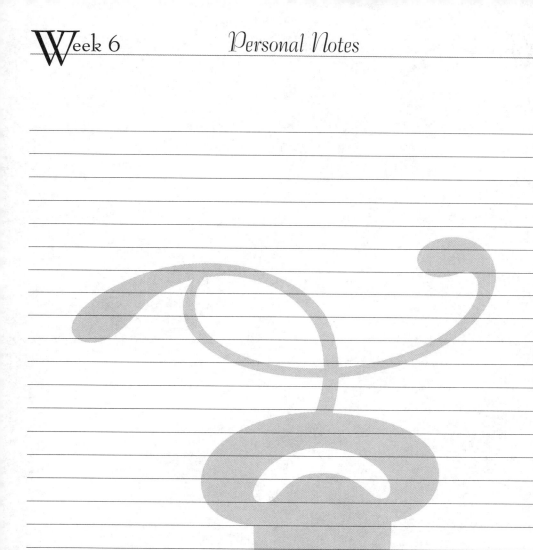

Personal Notes

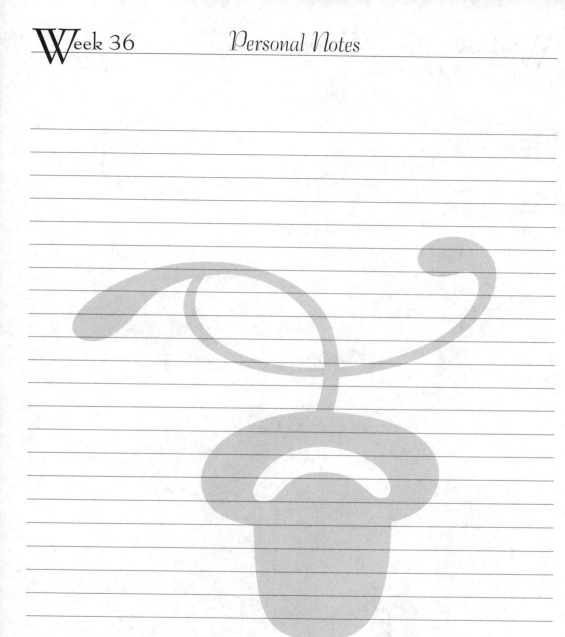

Personal Notes

Personal Notes

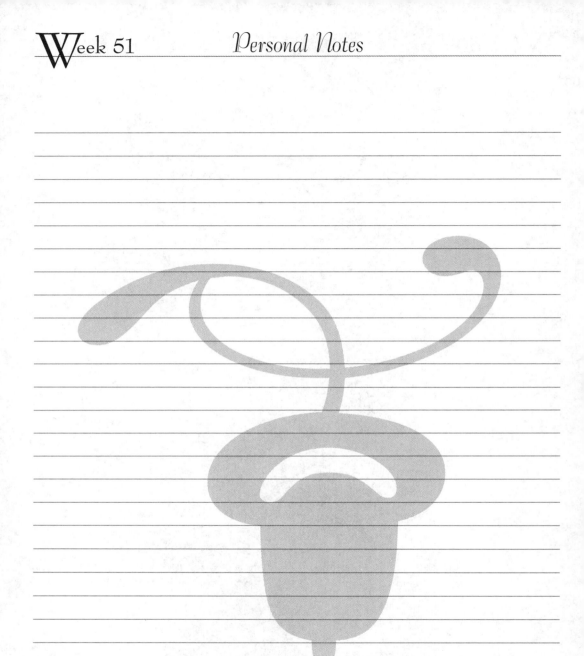

Week 52 Personal Notes

Telephone Numbers

Name _____

Address _____

_____

Telephone Number _____

Name _____

Address _____

_____

Telephone Number _____

Name _____

Address _____

_____

Telephone Number _____

Name _____

Address _____

_____

Telephone Number _____

Name _____

Address _____

_____

Telephone Number _____

Name _____

Address _____

_____

Telephone Number _____